365 Golf Quotes (A Golfing Quote for Every Day of the Year): For the Golfer Who Has Everything

Jackie Bolen

Copyright © 2023 by Jackie Bolen

All rights reserved. No part of this publication may be reproduced, distributed, or transmitted in any form or by any means, including photocopying, recording or other electronic or mechanical means without the prior written permission of the publisher, except in the case of brief quotations in critical reviews and certain other non-commercial uses permitted by copyright law. For permission requests, write to the publisher/author at the following address: Jackie Bolen: jb.business.online@gmail.com.

Table of Contents

January 4
February 9
March 13
April 18
May 23
June 28
July 32
August 37
September 42
October 47
November 52
December 57
Before You Go 62

January

January 1

"Golf is deceptively simple and endlessly complicated; it satisfies the soul and frustrates the intellect. It is at the same time rewarding and maddening—and it is without a doubt the greatest game mankind has ever invented." — Arnold Palmer

January 2

"The most important shot in golf is the next one." — Ben Hogan

January 3

"Golf is a game that is played on a five-inch course—the distance between your ears." — Bobby Jones

January 4

"It is almost impossible to remember how tragic a place this world is when one is playing golf." — Robert Wilson Lynd

January 5

"Golf is like a love affair. If you don't take it seriously, it's no fun; if you do take it seriously, it breaks your heart." — Arthur Daley

January 6

"Success in golf depends less on strength of body than upon strength of mind and character." — Arnold Palmer

January 7

"Golf is not just exercise; it's an adventure, a romance... a Shakespeare play in which disaster and comedy are intertwined." — Harold Segall

January 8

"Golf is a game of inches, miles, and moments. Each shot requires precision, perseverance, and a touch of magic." — Jack Nicklaus

January 9

"In golf as in life, it's the follow-through that makes the difference." — Unknown

January 10

"Golf is about how well you accept, respond to, and score with your misses much more so than it is a game of your perfect shots." — Dr. Bob Rotella

January 11

"Golf is a puzzle without an answer. I've played the game for 50 years, and I still haven't the slightest idea of how to play." — Gary Player

January 12

"Golf is a sport where success is determined by how well you manage failure." — Justin Rose

January 13

"To find a man's true character, play golf with him." — P.G. Wodehouse

January 14

"Golf is a sport of the open air in which everyone can participate, striving for perfection." — Arnold Palmer

January 15

"Golf is the closest game to the game we call life. You get bad breaks from good shots; you get good breaks from bad shots, but you have to play the ball where it lies." — Bobby Jones

January 16

"Golf is a game of skill, mental fortitude, and love for the challenge." — Tiger Woods

January 17

"Golf is a game that is played with the body, but won with the mind." — Greg Norman

January 18

"Golf is a beautiful and challenging journey, and each round is a story waiting to be written." — Lorena Ochoa

January 19

"Golf is a compromise between what your ego wants you to do, what experience tells you to do, and what your nerves let you do." — Bruce Crampton

January 20

"In golf, as in life, it's not the quantity but the quality of your shots that counts." — Tom Watson

January 21
"I don't think it's healthy to take yourself too seriously." — Payne Stewart

January 22
"Golf is not a game of great shots. It's a game of the most misses." — Ben Hogan

January 23
"Golf is a game of patience, persistence, and perspiration." — Darren Clarke

January 24
"The most important thing I've learned in golf is to remain humble, regardless of success or failure." — Davis Love III

January 25
"Golf is a game of respect and sportsmanship; we have to respect its traditions and its rules." — Jack Nicklaus

January 26
"Golf is a game where the ball lies poorly, and the players well." — Art Rosenbaum

January 27
"The least things upset him on the links. That last missed short putt was because of the uproar of the butterflies in the adjoining meadow." — PG Wodehouse

January 28
"The most rewarding things you do in life are often the ones that look like they cannot be done." — Arnold Palmer

January 29

"If profanity had an influence on the flight of the ball, the game of golf would be played far better than it is." — Horace G. Hutchinson

January 30

"Golf is a day spent in a round of strenuous idleness." — William Wordsworth

January 31

"Golf is about how well you can hit your second shot." — Jack Nicklaus

February

February 1
"Golf is not a sport, it's a lifestyle. Once you're in, you're in for life." — Unknown

February 2
"If a lot of people gripped a knife and fork the way they do a golf club, they'd starve to death." — Sam Snead

February 3
"What other people may find in poetry or art museums, I find in the flight of a good drive." — Arnold Palmer

February 4
"The golf swing is like a suitcase into which we are trying to pack one too many things." — John Updike

February 5
"Golf is not, on the whole, a game for realists. By its exactitude's of measurements, it invites the attention of perfectionists." — Heywood Hale Broun

February 6

"Golf is a good walk spoiled." — Mark Twain

February 7

"If you wish to hide your character, do not play golf." — Percy Boomer

February 8

"Golf is not just an exercise; it's an adventure, a romance, and a comedy all rolled into one." — Sir Winston Churchill

February 9

"Golf is a game that demands more than mastery of the physical self. It is a game of the soul." — Dr. DeForest Clinton Jarvis

February 10

"Golf is a game in which you yell 'fore,' shoot six, and write down five." — Paul Harvey

February 11

"Golf is a search for perfection, for balance. It's about meditation and concentration." — Greg Norman

February 12

"Golf tips are like Aspirin: One may do you good, but if you swallow the whole bottle you'll be lucky to survive." — Harvey Penick

February 13

"Golf is a game that reveals the character of a person." — Arnold Palmer

February 14

"My swing is so bad, I look like a caveman killing his lunch." — Lee Trevino

February 15

"Golf is the most fun you can have with your clothes on." — Chi Chi Rodriguez

February 16

"Golf is a fascinating game that has taken me to some of the most beautiful places." — Nancy Lopez

February 17

"Golf is about integrity. It reveals your character and how you handle adversity." — Fred Couples

February 18

"You've got to have the guts not to be afraid to screw up." — Fuzzy Zoeller

February 19

"Golf is a mental game. You are only as good as your last swing." — Hal Sutton

February 20

"Golf is the only sport I know of where a player pays for every mistake." — Al Geiberger

February 21

"Golf is a sport that cannot be perfected, only played better." — Bagger Vance (from the movie The Legend of Bagger Vance)

February 22

"Golf appeals to the idiot in us and the child. Just how childlike golfers become is proven by their frequent inability to count past five." — John Updike

February 23

"Tempo is the glue that sticks all elements of the golf swing together." — Nick Faldo

February 24

"Don't play too much golf. Two rounds a day are plenty." — Harry Valdon

February 25

"Golf is the hardest game in the world. There is no way you can ever get it. Just when you think you do, the game jumps up and puts you in your place." — Ben Crenshaw

February 26

"Golf is a game of precision, patience, and the pursuit of perfection. It's a timeless journey of self-discovery." — Byron Nelson

February 27

"Golf is a unique blend of science and art, where the player becomes the artist of their own destiny with every swing." — Greg Norman

February 28

"Golf is a humbling sport; it teaches you both the agony of defeat and the thrill of victory within the span of a few swings." — Annika Sörenstam

March

March 1

"Golf is not just a game; it's an obsession, a beautiful addiction that keeps us coming back for more." — Tom Watson

March 2

"Golf is a game where you compete not only against your opponents but against yourself and the course. It's a battle of wills and skill." — Peter Jacobsen

March 3

"Golf is a lifetime pursuit, a sport that challenges you physically, mentally, and spiritually. It's a journey that never ends." — Gary Player

March 4

"Golf is a game that tests your character, challenges your resilience, and humbles you in the pursuit of excellence." — Lee Trevino

March 5

"Golf is a game of rhythm and tempo, where the symphony of your swing determines the melody of your round." — Jack Nicklaus

March 6

"Golf is a sport that celebrates individuality, embraces diversity, and unites people from all walks of life on the same fairways." — Unknown

March 7

"Golf is a sport that teaches us to be better people—more patient, more humble, and more appreciative of the beauty around us." — Lorena Ochoa

March 8

"Golf is a sport that celebrates the beauty of competition, the joy of camaraderie, and the pursuit of excellence." — Steve Ballesteros

March 9

"Golf is a sport where success is measured not only in victories but in the lessons learned and the memories made." — Tom Kite

March 10

"If you break 100, watch your golf. If you break 80, watch your business." — Joey Adams

March 11

"They call it golf because all the other four letter words were taken." — Raymond Floyd

March 12

"Golf is a lot of walking, broken up by disappointment and bad arithmetic." — Unknown

March 13

"The only thing a golfer needs is more daylight." — Ben Hogan

March 14

"Golf is a game where guts and blind devotion will always net you absolutely nothing but an ulcer." — Tommy Bolt

March 15

"I look into eyes, shake their hand, pat their back, and wish them luck, but I am thinking, I am going to bury you." — Steve Ballesteros

March 16

"Golf is a game in which you claim the privileges of age and retain the playthings of childhood." — Samuel Johnson

March 17

"The reason I practice so much is so I can enjoy the essence of golf, which is being on the course." — Julius Boros

March 18

"Golf is a fascinating game that has taken me to some of the most beautiful places. Unfortunately, all of them are bunkers." — Unknown

March 19

"The ardent golfer would play Mount Everest if somebody put a flagstick on top." — Pete Dye

March 20

"The only time my prayers are never answered is on the golf course." — Billy Graham

March 21

"Golf is a game where white men can dress up as black pimps and get away with it." — Robin Williams

March 22

"Golf is the adult version of an Easter Egg Hunt." — Unknown

March 23

"They say golf is like life, but don't believe them. Golf is more complicated than that." — Gardner Dickinson

March 24

"Golf is so much about how you react, how you handle your mistakes. It's about managing your emotions and your game at the same time." — Lorena Ochoa

March 25

"Sometimes you win, sometimes you learn." — Unknown

March 26

"Golf is a game where you create your own path, overcome obstacles, and celebrate each small victory." — Inbee Park

March 27

"Golf is not just about hitting the ball, it's about how you think about hitting the ball." — Annika Sörenstam

March 28

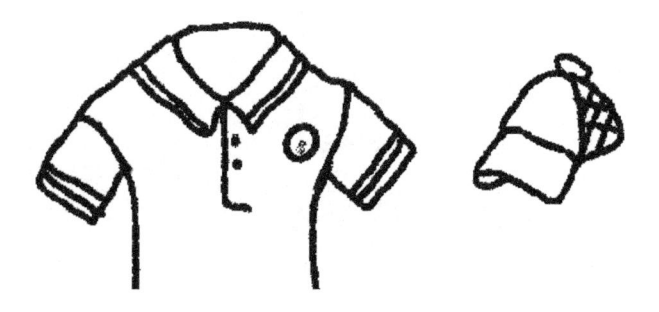

"You learn more from losing than winning. You learn how to keep going." — Morgan Pressel

March 29

"Golf is a way to connect with nature, with friends, with family. It's a beautiful sport that brings people together." — Michelle Wie

March 30

"Every defeat, every heartbreak, every loss, contains its own seed, its own lesson on how to improve your performance the next time." — Og Mandino

March 31

"Golf is a sport that requires patience, resilience, and a sense of humor—especially when the ball doesn't go where you want it to!" — Patty Sheehan

April

April 1

"Losing is not my enemy, fear of losing is my enemy." — Rafael Nadal

April 2

"Golf is a mental game. It's about staying focused, being in the moment, and not getting too high or too low." — Karrie Webb

April 3

"You have to accept your failures as well as your successes; you can't run from them, you can't hide from them. You have to face them." — Phil Mickelson

April 4

"Golf is a sport that rewards hard work, perseverance, and the ability to bounce back from setbacks." — Angela Stanford

April 5

"Golf is a game where you need to be patient and persistent, always striving to improve and enjoying the journey along the way." — Se Ri Pak

April 6

"I have failed again and again throughout my life. That's why I've been successful." — Michael Jordan

April 7

"Golf is a game of strategy and creativity, where you need to think your way through each round." — Karrie Webb

April 8

"I never learned anything from a match I won." — Bobby Jones

April 9

"Golf is a game that tests not only your physical skills but your mental strength and emotional composure as well." — Cristie Kerr

April 10

"Losing doesn't eat at me the way it used to. I just get ready for the next thing, the next fight. It's not about losing; it's about getting the right opportunity and taking it." — Rory McIlroy

April 11

"Golf is a sport that challenges you to focus on the present and let go of the past, shot by shot." — Lexi Thompson

April 12

"Golf is about perseverance and passion. It's about always pushing yourself to be better than you were yesterday." — Yani Tseng

April 13
"You can learn a line from a win and a book from a defeat." — Paul Brown

April 14
"Golf is a game where you learn to manage your expectations and stay resilient through every swing." — So Yeon Ryu

April 15
"Golf is a sport where you have to stay patient and trust the process. It's a game of inches and details." — Lexi Thompson

April 16
"Losing is a learning experience. It teaches you humility. It teaches you to work harder. It's also a powerful motivator." — Yani Tseng

April 17
"Golf is a sport where you learn to stay calm and composed, no matter the situation or the score." — Lydia Ko

April 18
"Golf is a game that teaches you humility and respect for the rules and for your fellow competitors." — Inbee Park

April 19
"You don't win tournaments by playing well and thinking poorly." — Bobby Jones

April 20
"Golf is a sport that teaches you to embrace challenges, to learn from failures, and to celebrate victories, big or small." — Lydia Ko

April 21

"Losses have propelled me to even bigger places, so I understand the importance of losing. You can never get complacent because a loss is always around the corner." — Venus Williams

April 22

"Golf is a game where you never stop learning, never stop improving, and never stop loving the challenge." — Pernilla Lindberg

April 23

"Golf is a beautiful sport that allows you to connect with nature and appreciate the beauty of the course." — Ariya Jutanugarn

April 24

You have to be able to accept failure to get better." — LeBron James

April 25

"Golf is a sport that teaches you the importance of precision and attention to detail in every aspect of your game." — Cristie Kerr

April 26

"Golf is a game that rewards hard work, dedication, and a never-give-up attitude." — Stacy Lewis

April 27

"Defeat is not the worst of failures. Not to have tried is the true failure." — George Edward Woodberry

April 28

"Golf is a journey of self-discovery, a constant pursuit of excellence and self-improvement." — Brooke Henderson

April 29

"Sometimes you're just happy to be out there and enjoy the game. But losing motivates me more." — Serena Williams

April 30

"Golf is a game where you have to stay positive, believe in yourself, and never give up, no matter the circumstances." — Jin Young Ko

May

May 1

"The only way to overcome loss is to learn from it." — Arnold Palmer

May 2

"Golf is a sport where you compete against yourself, constantly striving to be the best version of you on the course." — Danielle Kang

May 3

"I embrace losing as much as I embrace winning because they are both part of the journey." — Lexi Thompson

May 4

"Golf is a game where you have to trust yourself and your abilities, even when the pressure is high." — Jessica Korda

May 5

"It's not about how you handle the wins; it's about how you handle the losses." — Jack Nicklaus

May 6

"Golf is a sport that allows you to find balance, both physically and mentally, on the course and in life." — Jessica Korda

May 7

Watching Phil Mickelson play golf is like watching a drunk chasing a balloon near the edge of a cliff." — David Feherty

May 8

"Losses can make you stronger if you face them with courage, learn from them, and adapt." — Greg Norman

May 9

"Golf is a game where you need to be disciplined and committed to achieving your goals, one swing at a time." — Nelly Korda

May 10

"Golf is a game that challenges you to be strategic, to think ahead, and to adapt to changing circumstances." — Paula Creamer

May 11

"A loss is not a failure unless you make the same mistake twice." — John C. Maxwell

May 12

"If you're caught on a golf course during a storm and are afraid of lightning, hold up a 1-iron. Not even God can hit a 1-iron." — Lee Trevino

May 13

"Losing a game is heartbreaking. Losing your sense of excellence or worth is a tragedy." — Joe Paterno

May 14

"Golf is a sport that teaches you discipline and focus, qualities that are valuable both on and off the course." — Cristie Kerr

May 15

"A defeat is not the bitter end unless you allow it to be." — Bruce Lee

May 16

"Golf is a game that reminds you to always respect the rules, respect the course, and respect your competitors." — Ariya Jutanugarn

May 17

"Golf is a game that allows you to escape and connect with nature while testing your skill and determination." — Morgan Pressel

May 18

"You don't measure yourself by what you have accomplished, but by what you should have accomplished with your ability." — John Wooden

May 19

"Golf is a game of grace and precision, where each swing is a ballet of power and control." — Louise Suggs

May 20

"Every loss is a lesson. Learn it and move on. It's just one step closer to winning." — Annika Sörenstam

May 21

"Golf is a sport where every round is a chance to set a new personal record and push your limits." — Mirim Lee

May 22

"You never really lose until you stop trying." — Mike Ditka

May 23

"Golf is a sport that allows you to be yourself, express yourself, and enjoy the freedom of the fairways." — Amy Yang

May 24

"Golf is a journey that teaches you the importance of patience and persistence, on and off the course." — Jeongeun Lee

May 25

"Winning is great, sure, but if you are really going to do something in life, the secret is learning how to lose." — Wilma Rudolph

May 26

"Golf is a game where your passion for improvement fuels your desire to keep playing and keep getting better." — Jiyai Shin

May 27

"In defeat, you learn so much more about yourself than you do in victory." — Billy Casper

May 28

"Golf is a game of whispers—sometimes the wind shares its secrets." — Unknown

May 29

"Golf is a game where you create your own path, overcome obstacles, and celebrate each small victory." — Inbee Park

May 30

"In golf, the best shots are played with the heart." — Patti Blackstaffe

May 31

"Golf is a game of focus, patience, and endurance. It's a journey that teaches you valuable life lessons." — Moriya Jutanugarn

June

June 1

"Golf is a symphony, and the swing is its melody." — Moe Norman

June 2

"Golf is a sport where you aim for the stars, but sometimes you hit the trees." — Unknown

June 3

"Golf is like life—what matters is the journey, not the destination." — Gary McCord

June 4

"Golf is a game where you chase perfection but embrace imperfection." — Unknown

June 5

"The more I practice, the luckier I get." — Gary Player

June 6

"Golf is a game whose aim is to hit a very small ball into an even smaller hole, with weapons singularly ill-designed for the purpose." — Winston S. Churchill

June 7

"Golf is the poetry of motion." — R.H. Forsyth

June 8

"Golf is a game that humbles the mighty and exalts the meek." — Unknown

June 9

"Life is not fair, so why should I make a course that is fair." — Pete Dye

June 10

"Golf is a quest, a pursuit of something better, something deeper." — Unknown

June 11

"Golf is not a sport, it's a way of life." — Pete Dye

June 12

"Golf is a game where every shot is a fresh start." — Unknown

June 13

"Golf is a game of the heart and the mind, not just the body." — Lesley Garner

June 14

"Golf is a dance, and the course is your partner." — Unknown

June 15

"A bad attitude is worse than a bad swing." — Payne Stewart

June 16

"Master your short game. Chipping and putting mastery significantly lower your scores." — Tiger Woods

June 17

"Golf is a game that adds years to your life and life to your years." — Stan Smith

June 18

"Golf is a game where the past and the future merge in the present." — Unknown

June 19

"Golf is the art of thinking instead of straining." — Tommy Armour

June 20

"Golf is a game that whispers in the language of divots and putts." — Unknown

June 21

"Don't be too proud to take lessons. I'm not." — Jack Nicklaus

June 22

"Golf is a game where the smallest adjustments can yield the biggest results." — Unknown

June 23

"Golf is the only sport where the most feared opponent is you." — Tom Watson

June 24

"Golf is a game of strategy, disguised as a leisure activity." — Unknown

June 25

"Golf is the game you play against yourself, and sometimes it's the hardest opponent." — Mike Weir

June 26

"Golf is a journey of a thousand steps, each one leading you closer to your best swing." — Unknown

June 27

"Golf is a game that allows us to find peace in the chaos of life." — Muffin Spencer-Devlin

June 28

"Focus on fundamentals—grip, stance, posture, and alignment. A strong foundation sets the stage for success." — Jack Nicklaus

June 29

"Golf is a lot like taxes—what you don't understand is too expensive." — Joe Clark

June 30

"Perfect your grip; it's the foundation for a good swing. Spend time getting it right." — Ben Hogan

July

July 1

"Golf is a sport where you discover the world and yourself, one hole at a time." — Richard A. Mulligan

July 2

"Golf is a game where you can never conquer the course, but you can conquer yourself." — Unknown

July 3

"Golf is a riddle wrapped in an enigma, smothered in secret sauce." — Craig Magerkurth

July 4

"Golf is a conversation between you, the ball, and the course—a language only golfers understand." — Unknown

July 5

"Golf is a sport where you pay in sweat, time, and effort for your chances to laugh, smile, and enjoy the rewards." — Michael Ryan

July 6

"Golf is a game where the more you sweat in practice, the less you bleed in battle." — Unknown

July 7

"Swing smoothly and relaxed, focusing on tempo and rhythm. A tension-free swing leads to accuracy and distance." — Arnold Palmer

July 8

"Golf is the infallible test. The man who can go into a patch of rough alone, with the knowledge that only God is watching him, and play his ball where it lies, is the man who will serve you faithfully and well." — P.G. Wodehouse

July 9

"Golf is a sport that makes time stand still, at least until your ball lands in the water." — Unknown

July 10

"Stay fit and flexible. Fitness and flexibility are key for a consistent, powerful golf swing." — Gary Player

July 11

"Golf is a game where you strive for perfection, knowing you'll never quite reach it—and that's okay." — Unknown

July 12

"Focus on your balance. Maintain good balance and stability throughout the swing for control and power." — Rory McIlroy

July 13

"Golf is a sport that tests your patience, resilience, and sanity, all in 18 holes." — Unknown

July 14

"Master the flop shot—a finesse shot that's crucial in challenging situations on the course." — Phil Mickelson

July 15

"Golf is a game of inches, where every centimeter can make the difference between victory and defeat." — Unknown

July 16

"Keep your head still and your golf swing simple. Don't complicate your swing with unnecessary movements."— Sam Snead

July 17

"Golf is the only game where the worst player gets the best of it. He obtains more out of it in actual cash than the best player." — Arnold Haultain

July 18

"Golf is a game where your mind can wander, but your focus cannot." — Unknown

July 19

"Play for the love of the game, not just to conquer the course. Enjoy each round, regardless of the score." — Bobby Jones

July 20

"Visualize your shots and trust your instincts. Believe in your ability to execute each shot." — Steve Ballesteros

July 21

"Golf is a game where one good shot can erase a thousand bad ones, and one great round can erase a thousand bad days." — Unknown

July 22

"Find your natural swing and stick with it. Don't try to copy others; play the game that fits you best." — Lee Trevino

July 23

"The difference in golf and government is that in golf you can't improve your lie." — George Deukmejian

July 24

"Golf is the only game where the best player gets the fewest strokes." — Unknown

July 25

"Golf combines two favorite American pastimes: taking long walks and hitting things with a stick." — P.J. O'Rourke

July 26

"Practice your putting—more games are won and lost on the green. Master the art of the short game." — Tom Watson

July 27

"Golf is a game of whispers—listen closely, and the course will tell you its secrets." — Unknown

July 28

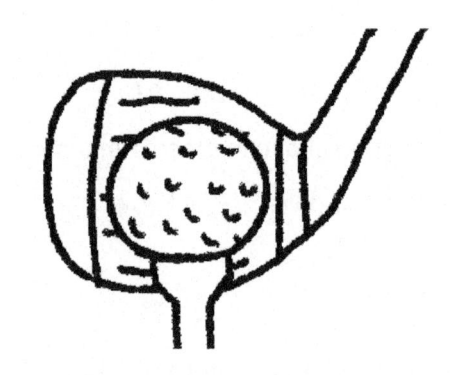

"Embrace the challenge of tough shots. Don't shy away from difficult situations; tackle them with confidence." — Padraig Harrington

July 29

"Golf is a puzzle with an infinite number of pieces, and just when you think you've solved it, a new piece appears." — Unknown

July 30

"Play with confidence and aggression. Believe in your abilities and play each shot with conviction." — Nancy Lopez

July 31

"Golf is a conversation between the soul and the swing." — Unknown

August

August 1

"Stay patient and maintain a sense of humor. Golf can be frustrating, but it's essential to keep a positive outlook." — Tommy Bolt

August 2

"Golf is a journey of endless discovery—of the self and the world around you." — Unknown

August 3

"Focus on course management. Play smart, make strategic decisions, and know when to take risks." — Greg Norman

August 4

"Golf is a game that evokes patience, perseverance, and the occasional profanity." — Unknown

August 5

"Perfect your pre-shot routine. Consistency begins with a consistent approach to each shot." — Payne Stewart

August 6

"Golf is a sport that lets you curse at a little white ball without offending anyone." — Unknown

August 7

"Control your tempo. A steady, well-paced swing is often more effective than a rushed one." — Tom Kite

August 8

"Golf is a game where you can't always control the outcome, but you can always control your effort." — Unknown

August 9

"Work on your posture. A good setup and posture can greatly influence the outcome of your swing." — Ernie Els

August 10

"Golf is a dance with nature, each swing a step in the choreography of the course." — Unknown

August 11

"Play one shot at a time. Don't get overwhelmed; focus on each shot in the present moment." — Nancy Lopez

August 12

"Golf is a sport that teaches you to celebrate the small victories—a well-placed chip, a clutch putt." — Unknown

August 13

"Mental preparation is key. Visualize your shots and scenarios before you step up to play." — Jordan Speith

August 14

"Golf is a sport where you can always blame your equipment, the weather, or your lucky socks." — Unknown

August 15

"Consistency is key. Work on maintaining a consistent swing and approach throughout the game." — Justin Rose

August 16

Golf is a game of strategy, where every shot is a move in the grand chess match with the course." — Unknown

August 17

"Short game saves scores. Spend extra time perfecting your chipping, pitching, and putting." — Gary Player

August 18

"Golf is a sport where you aim for the pin, but sometimes end up in the sand." — Unknown

August 19

"Understand the course. Study the layout, know the hazards, and plan your shots accordingly." — Lee Westwood

August 20

"Golf is a game where you chase a little white ball across acres of green and hope it doesn't find the rough." — Unknown

August 21

"Stay committed to your shots. Doubt can ruin a swing, so trust your decisions and follow through." — Stacy Lewis

August 22

"Golf is a journey that starts with excitement, often meanders through frustration, but occasionally lands in glory." — Unknown

August 23

"Believe in your swing. Confidence in your technique is crucial to executing each shot effectively." — Karrie Webb

August 24

"Golf is assuredly a mystifying game. It would seem that if a person has hit a golf ball correctly a thousand times, he should be able to duplicate the performance at will. But such is certainly not the case." — Bobby Jones

August 25

"Golf is a game that is structured on its most stupid feature—namely, the part that is played with the ball." — Gilbert K. Chesterton

August 26

"Never stop learning. Stay curious and open to new techniques and tips to improve your game." — Michelle Wie

August 27

"Golf is a good walk spoiled, but I'd rather be spoiling my walk than sitting in a car." — Alice Cooper

August 28

"Golf is a game in which you can drink and drive." — George Carlin

August 29

"Putt with feel and precision. Mastering your putting skills can significantly impact your overall performance." — Inbee Park

August 30

"Golf is a lot of walking, broken up by disappointment and bad arithmetic." — Unknown

August 31

"Golf is a game in which one endeavors to control a ball with implements ill adapted for the purpose." — Woodrow Wilson

September

September 1

"Adaptability is key. Adjust your game to different conditions and courses for better outcomes." — Kristie Kerr

September 2

"Golf is a fine relief from the tensions of office, but we are a little tired of holding the bag." — Charles Ervin

September 3

"Golf is a game where you can score six and still enjoy the 19th hole." — Unknown

September 4

"Work on mental strength. Stay focused, positive, and resilient even when facing challenges on the course." — Yani Tseng

September 5

"Golf is a passion that you spend your entire life being obsessed by, and even then you never quite figure it out." — Peter Jacobsen

September 6

"Golf is a game where you can enjoy instant gratification for a lifetime." — J. P. McEvoy

September 7

"Find your power source and use it. Understand what gives you distance and leverage that in your swing." — Brooke Henderson

September 8

"Golf is a sport where you can enjoy the great outdoors, like a walk in the park, with the added benefit of chasing a little white ball." — Unknown

September 9

"Keep your sense of humor. There's enough stress in the rest of your life not to let bad shots ruin a game you're supposed to enjoy." — Amy Alcott

September 10

"Don't be afraid to take risks strategically. Assess the situation and sometimes a bold shot pays off." — Lexi Thompson

September 11

"Golf teaches you patience, resilience, and the art of never giving up." — Unknown

September 12

"Golf is a reminder that in life, you may face rough patches, but you can always recover and move forward." — Unknown

September 13

"Golf is a sport where you learn to manage your expectations and stay resilient through every swing." — Unknown

September 14

"Own your game. Identify your strengths and build your strategy around them." — Stacy Lewis

September 15

"You miss 100% of the shots you don't take." — Wayne Gretzky

September 16

"Golf teaches you that success often comes from a series of small, consistent efforts." — Unknown

September 17

"Stay patient and trust the process. Progress in golf takes time, dedication, and resilience." — Lydia Ko

September 18

"It's not whether you get knocked down, it's whether you get up." — Vince Lombardi

September 19

"Golf teaches you to accept the consequences of your actions and make the best of the situation you're in." — Unknown

September 20

"Perfect your putting. A strong short game can significantly lower your scores." — Se Ri Pak

September 21

"Just keep going. Everybody gets better if they keep at it." — Ted Williams

September 22

"Golf teaches you to focus on the present moment and let go of past mistakes—an important lesson for life." — Unknown

September 23

"The more difficult the victory, the greater the happiness in winning." — Pelé

September 24

"Fitness matters. Work on strength and flexibility to improve your swing and endurance." — Cristie Kerr

September 25

"Golf teaches you that every round is a new opportunity to set a personal best." — Unknown

September 26

"You are never really playing an opponent. You are playing yourself, your own highest standards, and when you reach your limits, that is real joy." — Arthur Ashe

September 27

"Golf is a game that reminds you to always respect the rules, respect the course, and respect your competitors." — Unknown

September 28

"Learn from your mistakes. Analyze what went wrong in a bad shot, so you can avoid it in the future." —Jessica Korda

September 29

"In golf, as in life, you often face unexpected challenges. How you adapt to them defines your success." — Unknown

September 30

"To give any less than your best is to sacrifice a gift." — Steve Prefontaine

October

October 1
"Winning isn't everything, but wanting to win is." — Vince Lombardi

October 2
"Golf is a reminder that sometimes you need to take a step back to move forward and succeed." — Unknown

October 3
"You can't put a limit on anything. The more you dream, the farther you get." — Michael Phelps

October 4
"Golf is like hockey without the hits." — Wayne Gretzky

October 5
"Golf teaches you that practice and preparation are crucial for success, both on and off the course." — Unknown

October 6
"Champions keep playing until they get it right." — Billie Jean King

October 7

"In golf, you swing your best when you have the fewest things to think about." — Bobby Orr

October 8

"Golf is a game of honesty and integrity—a lesson in being true to yourself and others." — Unknown

October 9

"Do not let what you cannot do interfere with what you can do." — John Wooden

October 10

"Golf is a lot like hockey; it's all about that follow-through." — Mario Lemieux

October 11

"Persistence can change failure into extraordinary achievement." — Matt Biondi

October 12

"In golf, and in life, it's not about how many times you fall, but how many times you get up and try again." — Unknown

October 13

"Golf is a game that tests your patience and strategy, just like hockey." — Jaromir Jagr

October 14

"Make each day your masterpiece." — John Wooden

October 15

"Golf is so popular simply because it is the best game in the world at which to be bad." — A. A. Milne

October 16

"The difference between the impossible and the possible lies in a person's determination." — Tommy Lasorda

October 17

"Golf is like hockey—sometimes you need to take a power play and go for the long shot." — Bobby Clarke

October 18

"Success is where preparation and opportunity meet." — Bobby Unser

October 19

"Golf can best be defined as an endless series of tragedies obscured by the occasional miracle." — Unknown

October 20

"Hard work beats talent when talent doesn't work hard." — Tim Notke

October 21

"Stay true to yourself and listen to your inner voice. It will lead you to your dream." — James Ross

October 22

"Perseverance is not a long race; it is many short races one after another." — Walter Elliot

October 23

"Golf and hockey are both about balance—physical and mental." — Chris Chelios

October 24

"To succeed... you need to find something to hold on to, something to motivate you, something to inspire you." — Tony Dorsett

October 25

"If you think it's hard to meet new people, try picking up the wrong golf ball." — Jack Lemmon

October 26

"Winning takes precedence over all. There's no gray area. No almosts." — Kobe Bryant

October 27

"Golf is good for the soul. You get so mad at yourself you forget to hate your enemies." — Will Rogers

October 28

"The most rewarding things you do in life are often the ones that look like they cannot be done." — Arnold Palmer

October 29

"Success is not final, failure is not fatal: it is the courage to continue that counts." — Winston Churchill

October 30

"Golf is a thinking man's game. You can have all the shots in the bag, but if you don't know what to do with them, you've got troubles." — Chi Chi Rodriguez

October 31

"In golf, you take the shots you're given, just like in hockey, you take the opportunities presented to you." — Martin St. Louis

November

November 1
"Golf is a game, and games are meant to be enjoyed." — Raymond Floyd

November 2
"There is no such thing as natural touch. Touch is something you create by hitting millions of golf balls." — Lee Trevino

November 3
"Golf is a game of ego, but it is also a game of integrity: the most important thing is you do what is right when no one is looking." — Tom Watson

November 4
"Golf is a game where you can enjoy instant gratification for a lifetime." — J. P. McEvoy

November 5
"Golf is a sport that teaches you to celebrate the small victories—a well-placed chip, a clutch putt." — Unknown

November 6

"Golf is a game that's 90% mental and 10% mental." — Payne Stewart

November 7

"Golf is a game that is much more difficult to play than it is to spell." — Unknown

November 8

"Watching golf on television is like watching flies f***." - Lewis Black

November 9

"Golf is a game of disappointment, but still you return for the occasional good shot." — Unknown

November 10

"Golf is a fascinating game. It has taken me nearly forty years to discover that I can't play it." - Ted Ray

November 11

"I get to play golf for a living. What more can you ask for—getting paid for doing what you love." — Tiger Woods

November 12

"Golf is a game of emotion, exceptional scenery, and endearing relationships." — Unknown

November 13

"Golf is a game that unites your soul with the great outdoors." — Unknown

November 14

"No matter how good you get, you can always get better, and that's the exciting part." — Tiger Woods

November 15

"If you worry about making bogeys, it makes the game that much more difficult. You put more pressure on yourself without even noticing it. It makes a difference to take it easy when things aren't going right." — Sergio Garcia

November 16

"Golf is a game that allows you to chase perfection, knowing you'll never quite reach it—and that's okay." — Unknown

November 17

"Golf is evolving, every day is a new day, and I'm really interested in seeing how I can evolve and keep making it better." — Tiger Woods

November 18

"Golf is a game where the hazards don't move, but somehow you still manage to find them." — Unknown

November 19

"A good golfer has the determination to win and the patience to wait for the breaks." — Gary Player

November 20

"I'm not saying my golf game went bad, but if I grew tomatoes, they'd come up sliced." — Lee Trevino

November 21

"I think the guys who are really successful in this business [golf] have that killer instinct. They just want to win." — Tiger Woods

November 22

"Golf is a good walk, spoiled by a little white ball." — Alistair Cooke

November 23

"It's nice to put the green jacket on every once in a while, but I like to put the golf clubs in my hand a heck of a lot more." - Adam Scott

November 24

"In order to help people, you have to first learn how to help yourself, because you can't give away what you don't have." — Tiger Woods

November 25

"You don't have the game you played last year or last week. You only have today's game. It may be far from your best, but that's all you've got. Harden your heart and make the best of it." - Walter Hagen

November 26

"It is the most fascinating game, and the most fascinating part of it is that no matter how well or badly you play, it is a true test of yourself. You cannot fool yourself as you can in many other endeavors. You are either good, bad, or indifferent." - Bobby Jones

November 27

"Golf is a game that humbles the mighty and exalts the meek." — Unknown

November 28

"There's no such thing as bad weather, only inappropriate clothing!" — Unknown

November 29

"The real success is to play and come away with a victory when you are not on top form." — Jack Nicklaus

November 30

"I believe you can always come back. I've faced adversity before, and I've come back. It's about determination and persistence." — Tiger Woods

December

December 1

"I regard golf as an expensive way of playing marbles." — G.K. Chesterton

December 2

"Forget your opponents; always play against par." — Sam Snead

December 3

"Putts get real difficult the day they hand out the money." — Lee Trevino

December 4

"Golf, like measles, should be caught young." — P.G. Wodehouse

December 5

"The value of routine; trusting your swing." — Lorii Myers

December 6

"Never concede the putt that beats you." — Harry Vardon

December 7

"Every shot counts. The three-foot putt is as important as the 300-yard drive." — Henry Cotton

December 8

"The uglier a man's legs are, the better he plays golf. It's almost a law." — H.G. Wells

December 9

A perfectly straight shot with a big club is a fluke." — Jack Nicklaus

December 10

"You know what they say about big hitters...the woods are full of them." — Jimmy Demaret

December 11

"Golf: A plague invented by the Calvinistic Scots as a punishment for man's sins." — James Barrett Weston

December 12

"A shot that goes in the cup is pure luck, but a shot to within two feet of the flag is skill." — Ben Hogan

December 13

"When you lip out several putts in a row, you should never think that means that you're putting well. When you're putting well, the only question is what part of the hole it's going to fall in, not if it's going in." — Jack Nicklaus

December 14

"Although golf was originally restricted to wealthy, overweight Protestants, today it's open to anybody who owns hideous clothing." — Dave Berry

December 15

"The mind messes up more shots than the body." — Tommy Bolt

December 16
"The key to winning tournaments is consistent greatness, which is measured in victory points, not strokes." - Jack Nicklaus

December 17
"One of the most fascinating things about golf is how it reflects the cycle of life. No matter what you shoot – the next day you have to go back to the first tee and begin all over again and make yourself into something." — Peter Jacobsen

December 18
"You swing your best when you have the fewest things to think about." — Bobby Jones

December 19
"I don't let birdies and pars get in the way of having a good time" — Angelo Spagnolo

December 20
"It took me seventeen years to get three thousand hits in baseball. It took one afternoon on the golf course." — Hank Aaron

December 21
"Golf is not a game of good shots. It's a game of bad shots." - Ben Hogan

December 22
"Golf is a game you can never get too good at. You can improve, but you can never get to where you master the game." — Gay Brewer

December 23
"There are no shortcuts on the quest for perfection." — Ben Hogan

December 24

"Golf is the loneliest sport. You're completely alone with every conceivable opportunity to defeat yourself. Golf brings out your assets and liabilities as a person. The longer you play, the more certain you are that a man's performance is the outward manifestation of who, in his heart, he really thinks he is." — Hale Irwin

December 25

"As you walk down the fairway of life you must smell the roses, for you only get to play one round." — Ben Hogan

December 26

"Golf is the only sport I know of where a player pays for every mistake. A man can muff a serve in tennis, miss a strike in baseball, or throw an incomplete pass in football and still have another chance to square himself. In golf, every swing counts against you." — Lloyd Mangrum

December 27

"Concentration comes out of a combination of confidence and hunger." — Arnold Palmer

December 28

"You don't know what pressure is until you play for five bucks with only two bucks in your pocket." — Lee Trevino

December 29

"Mistakes are part of the game. It's how well you recover from them, that's the mark of a great player." — Alice Cooper

December 30

"Golf is a science, the study of a lifetime, in which you can exhaust yourself but never your subject." — David Forgan

December 31

"The secret of golf is to turn three shots into two." — Bobby Jones

Before You Go

If you enjoyed this book, please leave a review wherever you bought it! I'd really appreciate it.

You might also be interested in the following (also by Jackie Bolen):

- 500+ Would You Rather Questions for Adults

- Why Do We Say That? (For Adults)

Printed in Great Britain
by Amazon